Songs of Deliverance and Joy

Songs of Deliverance and Joy

The Ways of God in Grace

JOHN M. S. NEUFELD

Songs of Deliverance and Joy

Copyright © 2020 by John M. S. Neufeld. All rights reserved.

No part of this publication may be reproduced, stored in a retrieval system or transmitted in any way by any means, electronic, mechanical, photocopy, recording or otherwise without the prior permission of the author except as provided by USA copyright law.

The opinions expressed by the author are not necessarily those of URLink Print and Media.

1603 Capitol Ave., Suite 310 Cheyenne, Wyoming USA 82001
1-888-980-6523 | admin@urlinkpublishing.com

URLink Print and Media is committed to excellence in the publishing industry.

Book design copyright © 2020 by URLink Print and Media. All rights reserved.

Published in the United States of America

Libary of Congress Control Number: 2020918279
ISBN 978-1-64753-503-2 (Paperback)
ISBN 978-1-64753-504-9 (Hardback)
ISBN 978-1-64753-505-6 (Digital)

02.09.20

CONTENTS

To Jesus Now We Look 1
I Will Sing Of Thy Power 3
The Stones He Would Not Make 5
There He Sits Upon the Throne 7
The Day Is Fast Approaching 8
I Want To Walk With Thee 10
My Strength 13
In This World but Not a Part of It 15
Christ Jesus Saves and Delivers 17
The Needs Are Many 22
Dear Lord, It's Hard to Wait 24
Oh Sinner Hast Thou to Jesus Fled 26
Only Thou 28
The Waters 31
Give Us This Day 33
Surely He Hath Borne Our Griefs 35
If I Look Inward 38
As the Time Goes By 41
I Am a Blood-Washed Believer 44
My God Loves Me So 45
I Asked the Lord for a Soul to Touch 47
They Cried unto the Saviour 50
The Vessel Was Marred 52
I Know I Could Not Take it In 54
I Can Wait if I Must 56
This World is Rushing Headlong 58
Giving All to God 60

Not Now	62
Bless the Lord	63
There's a Man in the Glory	64
Could You Believe	66
The Emptiness Inside is Real	69
Love	70
In the Fullness of the Time	72
It is Finished	75
Jesus Will Not Fail Thee Ever	77
Not Two, but One	79
Oh Lord, Our Hearts Have Need of Peace	80
I Want to Go Home When It's Time	81
Oh to be Thankful	83
Give Thanks	85
It Couldn't be Long at All	86
Once I Was a Sinner	89
Forgetting That Which is Behind	90
Round the Lord	92
How I'm Doing	93
Restored	94
Jesus Reigns	96
Take It to Him	97
Too Much	98
See Him There	102
The Lord Doth Try the Hearts	104
Peter's Words	106
The Perfect Life of Jesus Christ	110
These Emblems	113
Stand Still	114
Today's the Day	116

We Fall Before Him	117
The Lord Will Come	119
Roses in December	120
As a Beacon of Light	121
The Patience of Job	123
You Know He's Jesus Christ	124
Some Handfuls of Purpose	126
Each Day in this Wilderness	128
We Walk by Faith	130
Jesus Himself Shall Descend	132
United	134
Victory	136
Faith	137
Take Heart	141
1980's Plea	142
Thou art Enough	145
Such Thy Love to Me	146
Christians First	149
Jesus Came	151
To Those Who Wait on God	152
Oh Lord, You Know I Need You	154
Faithful Warriors	155
Oh Wretched Man that I Am	156
Oh Lord, We Long to Follow Thee	157
The Storm May Full be Raging	160
How He Leads Them On	162
What if the Lord Should Come Before?	164
The Old Testament Books	165
COVID's For Real. Eternity, Too!	168

HEBREWS 12:1, 2

Wherefore seeing we also are compassed about with so great a cloud of witnesses, let us lay aside every weight, and the sin which doth so easily beset us, and let us run with patience the race that is set before us, Looking unto Jesus the author and finisher of our faith; who for the joy that was set before him endured the cross, despising the shame, and is set down at the right hand of the throne of God

To Jesus Now We Look

To Jesus now we look,
The author of our faith;
We all await His soon return,
All who are saved by grace.

He lived, a perfect man,
As God, from sin removed;
Made manifest the Father's heart,
To end His own He loved.

My peace I give to you.
Let not your hearts e'er fret;
Not as the world, He said He'd give,
Full peace, and without let.

Man mocked our blessed Lord,
Abused His body sore;
Led Him to die upon the cross,
His hands with nails they bore.

'Twas He who did the work.
On Calv'ry gave His life;
Was left of God for three full hours,
Did bear our sins and grief.

Soon will He come again;
We then with Him shall be.
Forever blest with Christ our Head;
His bride eternally!!

PSALM 59:16

But I will sing of thy power; yea, I will sing aloud of thy mercy in the morning: for thou hast been my defence and refuge in the day of my trouble.

I Will Sing Of Thy Power

I will sing of Thy power
To save my very soul;
(2X) The Blood Thou sheddest in that hour
Has washed and made me whole.

Who but the Lamb of God
Could do a work as this?
(2X) To bow beneath God's heavy rod
Of wrath and righteousness.

None but our blessed Lord
Has ever shown such love;
(2X) Obedient to His Father's word,
He stooped from Heaven above.

Christ came in human flesh,
Yet ever sin apart;
(2X) And in such perfect holiness
Revealed the Father's heart.

All honour, praise and glory
To Jesus Christ, God's Son,
(2X) Who died to bear our sins away,
Yet He the spotless One.

He into death did go,
That we might never die.
(2X) Oh, who could ever love us so?
"All praise!" our hearts must cry!

MATTHEW 4:1-11

Then was Jesus led up of the Spirit into the wilderness to be tempted of the devil. And when he had fasted forty days and forty nights, he was afterward an hungred. And when the tempter came to him, he said, If thou be the Son of God, command that these stones be made bread. But he answered and said, It is written, Man shall not live by bread alone, but by every word that proceedeth out of the mouth of God. Then the devil taketh him up into the holy city, and setteth him on a pinnacle of the temple, And saith unto him, If thou be the Son of God, cast thyself down: for it is written, He shall give his angels charge concerning thee: and in their hands they shall bear thee up, lest at any time thou dash thy foot against a stone. Jesus said unto him, It is written again, Thou shalt not tempt the Lord thy God. Again, the devil taketh him up into an exceeding high mountain, and sheweth him all the kingdoms of the world, and the glory of them; And saith unto him, All these things will I give thee, if thou wilt fall down and worship me. Then saith Jesus unto him, Get thee hence, Satan: for it is written, Thou shalt worship the Lord thy God, and him only shalt thou serve. Then the devil leaveth him, and, behold, angels came and ministered unto him.

The Stones He Would Not Make

The stones He would not make
To be bread for His food;
Nothing here could He take,
But by the Word of God.

Himself He would not cast
From off the temple spire;
To tempt His God, alas,
Did Satan thus require.

Nor would the Holy One
Fall at the devil's feet.
The Lord your God alone
Of worshipping is meet.

Such power and love displayed,
Our hearts with praises ring.
Sin's wages have been paid —
Where now, O Death, thy sting?

REVELATION 3:21

To him that overcometh will I grant to sit with me in my throne, even as I also overcame, and am set down with my Father in his throne.

There He Sits Upon the Throne

There He sits upon the throne,
All redemption's work is done.
Christ the ransom to atone
Is set as the Cornerstone.

Glory to the Lamb of God,
Who this scene of sorrow trod;
Bowed beneath God's righteous rod,
Purged our sins with His own blood.

Praise we to the Father sing,
Bow with full hearts worshipping,
For the blessings Christ doth bring
To His own in everything.

See the Son with glory crowned,
At the Father's side enthroned.
All the lost He sought and found,
Led them to redemption's ground.

The Day Is Fast Approaching

The day is fast approaching,
When we'll be home at last;
And all our woes and sorrows
Will then be over past.
We wait the day with trembling,
And pray it will be near.
Oh that we might be faithful,
And found in godly fear.

Thy Name this world blasphemeth,
Thy grace it doth despise,
And to Thy blest salvation
Vile hatred thence doth rise.
Dear Lord, we know our portion
In flames with them had been,
Had Thou not called us to Thee
By Thy great love supreme.

We wait that glorious day, Lord,
When we shall hear Thy shout
With angel's voice and God's trump,
To call Thy chosen out;
Then will we leave this scene, Lord,
To meet Thee in the air;
At last to see Thee, Saviour,
In all Thy glory fair.

I need Thee, blessed Saviour,
I crave Thy tender touch.
Please grant Thy calming presence,
O Thou Who lovest much.
When by the foe surrounded,
With fear on every side,
Lord, help me more to trust Thee,
And in Thy fear abide.

I Want To Walk With Thee

I want to walk with Thee,
O Saviour, please let it be;
Here where Thy pathway led
'Midst sin and iniquity;
To walk in Thy footsteps,
In this scene Thou hast trod;
Lord Jesus help me to follow,
And live my life for God.

I want to walk with Thee
Wherever the road may lead;
I want to live for Thee,
Lord, this is my deepest need —
To walk more closely,
And live more wholly
Devoted unto Thee;
I want to walk with Thee
Until Thy blest face I see.

*The author was crying out to the Lord
On his bed in 1985,
"I want to walk with Thee,
I want to walk with Thee!"
Then the words to this poem came to him.*

PSALMS 18:1-3

*I will love thee, O Lord, my strength.
The Lord is my rock, and my fortress, and my deliverer;
my God, my strength, in whom I will trust; my buckler,
and the horn of my salvation, and my high tower.
I will call upon the Lord, who is worthy to be praised:
so shall I be saved from mine enemies.*

My Strength

My Strength, my Rock, my Fortress,
My Deliverer, my God, my Rock,
My Buckler, the Horn of my Salvation,
And my High Tower;
My Strength, my Rock, my Fortress,
My Deliverer, my God, my Rock,
My Buckler, the Horn of my Salvation,
And my High Tower.

I will call upon the Lord,
Who is worthy to be praised.
So shall I be saved
From my enemies.

My Strength, my Rock, my Fortress,
My Deliverer, my God, my Rock,
My Buckler, the Horn of my Salvation,
And my High Tower;
My Buckler, the Horn of my Salvation,
And my High Tower.

JOHN 17:13-17

*And now come I to thee; and these things I speak in the world,
that they might have my joy fulfilled in themselves.
I have given them thy word; and the world hath hated them,
because they are not of the world, even as I am not of the world.
I pray not that thou shouldest take them out of the world,
but that thou shouldest keep them from the evil.
They are not of the world, even as I am not of the world.
Sanctify them through thy truth: thy word is truth.*

In This World but Not a Part of It

1
In this world, but not a part of it,
Called to touch the very heart of it,
Rescue souls from the deep and miry pit,
Preaching Christ to the lost.

CHORUS
For we were foreknown long before the earth was made,
Predestinated to a time and place,
Called to Him by His own sovereign grace,
Justified, then glorified as His Bride.

2
Christ's shed blood has washed us from all sin.
A new life in Him we now begin.
Realizing how it might have been,
Had He not poured it out.

CHORUS

3
If this world has no warm place for you,
Know full well it had none for Jesus too.
You'll find blessing if to Him you're true.
We're not a part of this world.

CHORUS

The words of this song,
And the previous,
Are believed to be the earliest
Of the author's writings.
Around 1981/82

Christ Jesus Saves and Delivers

CHORUS
Christ Jesus saves and delivers
From sin, and its chains and fetters;
Our faith alone stands on God's Son,
Who died and rose the third day.

1

He was born of the virgin Mary,
All of God's angels witness bearing;
And He walked holy, perfect, before God's face,
Amongst His very own;
He came a light into this world
Which all refused to see;
Had He not come in grace and truth,
We still undone would be.

CHORUS

2

Our hope is in our Saviour,
And we rejoice in His great favour,
Knowing that He for us in the flesh did come
To please a Holy God;
He was obedient unto death,
And that upon the Cross,
And He, the Ruler of the worlds,
For us did suffer loss.

CHORUS

3
He was bruised for our transgressions,
That we might receive many blessings,
And He was left of God on th'accursed Cross,
That we might all draw nigh.
Salvation was completed,
And the debt was fully paid:
Our great High Priest and Mercy Seat
The full atonement made.

CHORUS

4
We spread abroad His glory,
And we tell everyone the story,
How that He suffered under the hand of God
And bore His righteous wrath-
A wrath so kindled by our sins
Which cried to Him so sore;
But now love reigns, for Christ did bear it
Till there was no more.

CHORUS

5
Our sins have full forgiveness,
And His own precious blood does cleanse us;
If we just put our faith in His finished work,
His Spirit will be ours.
We then shall walk in a brand new life,
A life from deep within,
For we are dead and raised with Christ,
No more to live in sin.
CHORUS

6
If our conscience needs some purging,
Know it's Christ's Holy Spirit's urging,
That we just read our Bibles and pray in faith
To cleanse us from our guilt;
Our unconfessed transgressions can
Communion surely break,
But nought eternal life in Christ
From us can ever take!

CHORUS

7
We glory in our testings,
Knowing that they result in patience,
Being of much more value than gold, though tried
In Satan's hottest fires;
He hopes the trials he puts us through
Will prove our uselessness,
But they're God's tools to humble us
And free us of our flesh.

CHORUS

8
Behold, how much the Father
Shows us His heart's love like no other,
In that we here now children of God are called,
And soon shall be like Him.
We wait for His returning soon,
When with a shout so loud,
Th'Archangel will us give the call
To meet Him in the cloud.

CHORUS

Has the reader met the Lord Jesus
as their own personal, loving Saviour?
Today is not too late!

The Needs Are Many

Needs are many great and varied
In this lost and dying world.
Who will preach a risen Saviour
Through the Bible's truth unfurled?

CHORUS

Preach the Gospel,
Spread the message
Of a Saviour's dying love.

2
Oh the needy, hungry masses
Dying for that living bread:
Could we fail to feed them fully,
Ere their soul be lost and dead?

CHORUS

3
Are there any who are willing
Ease and comfort to resign,
In obedience and submission
To the Master's great design?

CHORUS

4
Preach the Gospel, spread the message
Of a Saviour's dying love;
He who came a ransom paying
Captive souls to bring above.

CHORUS

5
Have we found a full salvation
Rescued from the snares of sin?
Oh then let us tell the story,
Rescue souls and bring them in.

CHORUS

6
All may not be called to service
Far from home and family dear;
All may preach a risen Saviour,
Live their lives in godly fear.

CHORUS

Dear Lord, It's Hard to Wait

Dear Lord, it's hard to wait on Thy good time:
My faith it often fails, when I see no reason or rhyme.
Please teach me now to pray and trust Thy Holy Word,
For I know all is well, when I lean on Christ my Lord.

*Patience in all aspects of life is most needed
by the saints of God, and is a quality in which the Lord
delights to instruct them. When we fail to wait on Him, our
impatience often brings consequences intended to drive us back
to His dear loving arms. God's timing is perfect timing.*

PSALM 27:14

Says:
Wait on the Lord: be of good courage,
and He will strengthen your heart;
wait, I say, on the Lord.

Oh Sinner Hast Thou to Jesus Fled

Oh sinner, hast thou to Jesus fled for safety?
He Who His own life lost to save thee,
Made sin that He might righteous make thee,
Cleanse thee from all guilt.
This Jesus came from the heights of glory down
To earth and as humble man was found,
And gave Himself a ransom for thy sins.

The Saviour stands at thy heart's door,
Rich blessings would outpour.
Please open to Jesus Christ
While 'tis the day of grace:
Thou knowest not what another day may bring
Of God's righteous judgment, or death's sting;
Today is the day when thou must choose,
Today is the day when thou must choose.

*This song was originally written
To be sung in two breaths.*

Only Thou

Only Thou, Lord Jesus Christ,
Canst cleanse us from all sin;
Only Thou and Thou alone
Canst give us peace within.

None but thee can satisfy,
We need Thee every day.
Flesh, the world, the devil too
Would have us as their prey.

Unto Thee and Thee alone
Our eyes must ever gaze:
Else we stumble in the dark,
Or stray from Thy blest ways.

Ever just to Thee we'd flee,
When trials press us sore;
Refuge of the needy soul,
Thy grace Thou dost outpour.

Nought but Thy surpassing love
Could keep us close to Thee;
Only in Thy arms secure
Would we contented be.

God the Father, Thee we thank,
Christ Jesus, Lord, would praise;
For the Holy Ghost, Thy gift,
Our Guide through pilgrim days.

Thou didst give us such a place
As only Thou could'st, Lord:
One with God eternally;
'Tis written in Thy Word.

2 Peter 1: 1-4
Simon Peter, a servant and an apostle of Jesus Christ, to them that have obtained like precious faith with us through the righteousness of God and our Saviour Jesus Christ:Grace and peace be multiplied unto you through the knowledge of God, and of Jesus our Lord, According as his divine power hath given unto us all things that pertain unto life and godliness, through the knowledge of him that hath called us to glory and virtue: Whereby are given unto us exceeding great and precious promises: that by these ye might be partakers of the divine nature, having escaped the corruption that is in the world through lust.

EZEKIEL 47:3-6

And when the man that had the line in his hand went forth eastward, he measured a thousand cubits, and he brought me through the waters; the waters were to the ankles. Again he measured a thousand, and brought me through the waters; the waters were to the knees. Again he measured a thousand, and brought me through; the waters were to the loins. Afterward he measured a thousand; and it was a river that I could not pass over: for the waters were risen, waters to swim in, a river that could not be passed over. And he said unto me, Son of man, hast thou seen this? Then he brought me, and caused me to return to the brink of the river.

The Waters

He brought me through the waters
  Which o'er my ankles flowed.
  The going was much harder,
  But I leaned on my God.
He brought me through the waters
  Which now were to my knees;
  My progress was much slower,
  His outstretched Hand I seized.

He brought me through the waters.
  My loins were covered then.
  I held my Saviour nearer,
  Went on with Him again;
He brought me through the waters,
  Too deep for me to stand:
  I could not cross the river,
  Nor swim toward dry land.

He brought me through these waters,
  As only He could do;
  My precious, loving Saviour,
  So faithful, and so true;
He brought me through the waters,
  Which overwhelmed my soul:
  And spoke, My child, take courage,
  For I am in control!

MATTHEW 6:11

Give us this day our daily bread.

Give Us This Day

Give us this day our daily bread,
Such as the need should be;
Lord we depend on Thee alone;
Thine eyes, O Lord, do see.
Our souls would be fed by Thee alone.
Our mouths say to Thee, Thy will be done.
Ever by Thee the battles won.
Now we look up to Thee.

Great is the need of Thy people, Lord,
Many and varied the cares.
Thou art aware of each burden, Lord,
As we bow down in prayer.
We pour them out at Thy feet, and trust.
Gladly bow down as we know we must.
Thou art, we own it, the Holy and Just,
Ever, always right there.

There is no other to whom we turn.
There is none else so near.
Keep us dependent, obedient still,
For Thou wilt soon appear.
Soon is the day of Thy coming, Lord.
What jubilation the thought affords!
Faith clings to Thee and Thy faithful Word.
Cause us Thy voice to hear!

ISAIAH 53

Who hath believed our report? and to whom is the arm of the Lord revealed? For he shall grow up before him as a tender plant, and as a root out of a dry ground: he hath no form nor comeliness; and when we shall see him, there is no beauty that we should desire him. He is despised and rejected of men; a man of sorrows, and acquainted with grief: and we hid as it were our faces from him; he was despised, and we esteemed him not. Surely he hath borne our griefs, and carried our sorrows: yet we did esteem him stricken, smitten of God, and afflicted. But he was wounded for our transgressions, he was bruised for our iniquities: the chastisement of our peace was upon him; and with his stripes we are healed. All we like sheep have gone astray; we have turned every one to his own way; and the Lord hath laid on him the iniquity of us all. He was oppressed, and he was afflicted, yet he opened not his mouth: he is brought as a lamb to the slaughter, and as a sheep before her shearers is dumb, so he openeth not his mouth. He was taken from prison and from judgment: and who shall declare his generation? for he was cut off out of the land of the living: for the transgression of my people was he stricken. And he made his grave with the wicked, and with the rich in his death; because he had done no violence, neither was any deceit in his mouth. Yet it pleased the Lord to bruise him; he hath put him to grief: when thou shalt make his soul an offering for sin, he shall see his seed, he shall prolong his days, and the pleasure of the Lord shall prosper in his hand. He shall see of the travail of his soul, and shall be satisfied: by his knowledge shall my righteous servant justify many; for he shall bear their iniquities. Therefore will I divide him a portion with the great, and he shall divide the spoil with the strong; because he hath poured out his soul unto death: and he was numbered with the transgressors; and he bare the sin of many, and made intercession for the transgressors.

Surely He Hath Borne Our Griefs

Surely He hath borne our griefs,
And carried our sorrows too;
Yet, we esteemed Him smitten of God,
Stricken, afflicted too.

For our transgressions came His wound,
Was bruised for iniquities;
Our peace's chastisement upon Him fell,
And with His stripes we are healed.

All we like sheep have gone astray
Turning each to their own way;
Th'iniquity of us all the Lord
Hath laid upon Him, blest word!

He was oppressed and afflicted,
He opened not His mouth.
Brought as a lamb to the slaughter,
As a sheep for the shearing, was dumb.

Taken from prison and judgment,
Who shall declare His seed?
Cut off from the land of the living,
For my people's transgressions was stricken.

He made His grave with the wicked,
Was with the rich in His death,
Because He had done no violence,
Nor was deceit found in His mouth.

Yet it pleased the Lord to bruise Him.
He hath put to grief that One.
His soul shall make an offering for sin.
He'll prolong His days and see His seed

The full pleasure of the Lord
Shall prosper in His hand;
He'll see the travail of His soul,
And shall be satisfied.

By knowledge my righteous Servant
Shall justify many unjust;
He shall bear their iniquities.
Man of sorrows, acquainted with grief

I'll divide Him a place with the great,
And He, the spoil with the strong;
Since He poured out His soul unto death,
And with the transgressors was numbered.

He bore the sins of many,
And for the transgressors prayed;
My servant exalted shall prosper,
Be extolled and made very high:
For He was despised and rejected,
And we hid our faces from Him.
Despis ed was He, we esteemed Him not
This Jesus, Messiah, God's Son.

*Let us pause to consider our blessed
Messiah's sufferings for our sakes!*`

If I Look Inward

If I look inward, Lord, I see
Such sin as none could know;
If I look round about Thy church,
Such weakness thence does flow.
Or, if at this sad faltering world
I cast about my gaze,
I see a lost and dying crowd
So ripe for judgment days.

My eyes are daily filled, O Lord,
I must needs look away;
But where, oh where, can one behold
What's right and just, I pray?
Is that Thy voice that bids me look
To Thee exalted high,
To see in Thee God's answer sure
For all that makes me sigh?

Oh yes! To gaze at Thee alone
Sets free from sin within,
Gives grace to bear my brother's load,
Convicts this world of sin;
Oh, by Thy spirits power I will!
Give grace, I pray, O Lord:
To walk by faith, and not by sight,
Believing in Thy Word.

Have we ever gotten our eyes off the Lord?

JOSHUA 5: 10-12

And the children of Israel encamped in Gilgal, and kept the passover on the fourteenth day of the month at even in the plains of Jericho. And they did eat of the old corn of the land on the morrow after the passover, unleavened cakes, and parched corn in the selfsame day. And the manna ceased on the morrow after they had eaten of the old corn of the land; neither had the children of Israel manna any more; but they did eat of the fruit of the land of Canaan that year.

As the Time Goes By

As the time goes by, and the day draws nigh
To Thy coming again to earth,
Keep us still in Thy Word, Holy blessed Lord,
That we lose not sight of its worth:
For the enemy seeks, through the days and the weeks
To turn our hearts from the goal,
While the world surrounds with its sights and its sounds,
And senses the flesh control.

'Tis Thyself alone that we worthy own
To guide us aright while we're here,
For the way is long, and we must be strong,
Or we'll be overcome by fear.
Thus we seek Thy face, and beseech Thy grace
For the pathway that leads ahead
To the Promised Land, where by faith we stand
Even now with our risen Head.

Oh, but while we wait for that nuptial date
When the Bridegroom at last we shall see,
We need to be fed with the heavenly bread
And to drink of the waters free;
Thus we feast on Christ, God's gift un-priced
From heaven to earth come down,
Who atonement made, and the ransom paid
By making our sins His own.

Our Passover Lamb is the Great I Am
Who suffered God's wrath in our place,
And our souls are fed with the unleavened bread
Of the sinless One's life and His grace;
The manna is got ere the sun rises hot,
And is measured to each as his need;
While the food of the land, and the corn in our hand
Show the bounty on which we can feed.

For us there's no lack, and there's no turning back;
We press on to the goal and the prize,
To the great upward call, to Christ Jesus our All,
Whom we'll meet face to face in the skies;
So, as the time presses on to that glorious dawn
Of the coming again of our Lord,
Let's keep close to His side, and in Him abide,
Still praying, and reading His Word.
Still praying, and reading His Word.

Lord I'm doing my best
To do what I can
To do what I must,
And I really must keep on going!
2x

Let's be ready for the Lord's return.

I Am a Blood-Washed Believer

I am a blood-washed believer in Messiah,
And I rejoice in the love He has for me.
Jehovah sent Him as promised in the Scriptures:
Yeshua came down to set His people free.

He lived a life that pleased Jehovah,
That He might be pleased with man again.
He bore my sins upon Golgotha,
And since He saved me He is my truest friend.

My God Loves Me So

My God loves me so,
My God's in control,

My God's still on my side,
He's a mighty Saviour!

I'll praise Jesus Christ,
God's Lamb for Sacrifice,

Who died to save me from sin.

Sharing the Gospel with others.

I Asked the Lord for a Soul to Touch

I asked the Lord for a soul to touch,
Be it ever so near or so far.
And He asked me had I been looking much
To see just where they all are?

So I said to myself
As I sat where I was,
"You know, there's a world that is full
Of souls that are dying,
And that, just because,
Some thought they were unreachable."

So now what to do when you're not really sure
Of the time or the place, or the words:
When set face to face with a soul insecure,
Just tell them that you are the Lord's.

In words plain and simple that come from a heart
That knows what it means to be free,
Explain how He saved you and set you apart
As His own for eternity.

For God is not hindered in saving that soul,
And He does it still, time and again;
Healing them, cleansing them, making them whole
In His love for the children of men.

So pray on, dear believer, and seek from His hand
A sense of His grace and His power;
Bring others to Heaven, though hell should withstand,
And He'll give you His strength for the hour.

JOHN 4: 39-42

And many of the Samaritans of that city believed on him for the saying of the woman, which testified, He told me all that ever I did. So when the Samaritans were come unto him, they besought him that he would tarry with them: and he abode there two days. And many more believed because of his own word; And said unto the woman, Now we believe, not because of thy saying: for we have heard him ourselves, and know that this is indeed the Christ, the Saviour of the world.

They Cried unto the Saviour

They cried unto the Saviour,
And He answered them, He did!
"I'll show you great and hidden things
Unknown by you", He said.

Lord, all my ways I have declared,
And Thou hast answered me;
Yet he who trusts shall not make haste:
Hence I need help from Thee.

His God does give discretion,
And does lead him in the way;
"Return, and rest, be still, and know
That I am God", He'd say.

Whatever be our future
Must in Thy hands be laid.
Our lives are Thine, and not our own,
So teach us, Lord, to wait.

In perfect peace and confidence
Shall be our strength, when we
Commit our lives, our hearts, our all
In faith, dear Lord, to Thee.

ISAIAH 30:15

For thus saith the Lord God, the Holy One of Israel; In returning and rest shall ye be saved; in quietness and in confidence shall be your strength...

The Vessel Was Marred

The vessel was marred in the hands of the Potter:
  Now what was the Potter to do?
Such plans for a vessel of exquisite beauty
  Could not now be so fully through.

He pondered awhile o'er that lump on the wheel:
  What could He? What would He now do?
Ah! And it dawned like a beautiful morn,
  He'd still make it beautiful, too!

He toiled through the night, 'til dawned a new day,
  Then stepped back and gasped in delight.
The vessel He viewed was a masterpiece now,
  That glistened and gleamed in the light.

Just what was the change that came over that lump,
  When yielded to His loving hands?
When lost in the wonder of His sculpting powers,
  And the knowledge that He understands.

The Lord is the Potter, and we are the clay:
  What He makes of us is no mistake.
Yet, if marred in His hands, in those marvelous hands,
  Still a vessel to blessing He'll make.

For God is not hindered in what He can do
  With a vessel that's yielded to Him.
As seems best to the Moulder of lives with His hands,
  He'll fashion it new, from within.

JEREMIAH 18:3,4

Then I went down to the potter's house, and, behold,
he wrought a work on the wheels.
And the vessel that he made of clay was marred in the hand of the potter: so
he made it again another vessel, as seemed good to the potter to make it.

I Know I Could Not Take it In

I know I could not take it in,
Nor understand God's ways with men;
I could not fathom all His plans
Through Christ, who walked below as Man.

But I can take it to His throne,
And there my human weakness own;
Confessing, as I kneel to pray,
His faithfulness, and perfect ways.

Then, why the doubts, the fears, the cares:
Don't I believe God answers prayer?
Does not my Lord and Saviour know
So perfectly my grief and woe?

If that be so, then I must cling
To God, by faith, through everything;
Though hell, the world, the flesh assail,
His promises will never fail.

He said He'd never leave, forsake
Those who Himself their refuge make:
"I'm with you always", was His pledge;
His presence known, our privilege.

So let us onward press toward home,
Expecting Jesus soon to come;
Our questions, and our burdens lay
At His blest feet, and watch, and pray!

Do we ever wonder what God is doing?

I Can Wait if I Must

I can wait, if I must,
For your precious love,
For I know I'll be blest:
So I'll read and I'll pray,
Look to Him every day,
As I let our dear Lord do the rest.

Like the Lord for His bride,
I waited for you,
Patiently day by day;
Through His grace well-sustained,
My heart was maintained,
By the love He bestowed on the way.

It was love sorely tried,
As we sought His face,
Wanting just His blest will;
We were cast on or knees,
Brought to Him all our pleas,
Knowing He our deep needs would fulfill.

So let's praise and adore
Our Lord evermore,
For His great faithfulness!
Having loved us so much,
He caused our lives to touch,
That we other lives, too, might bless.

Oh the depth of the love
Of our blessed Lord
Is beyond tongue to tell!
Let's return this great love
To that One up above;
Serving Him, who has made all things well.

This World is Rushing Headlong

This world is rushing headlong
On a steady path to hell,
Heeding not the gracious gospel
God has sent the Church to tell;
Of a merciful Redeemer
Who His precious Blood did shed,
That a sinner, though so guilty,
Might be justified instead.

Justified, and not condemned,
Could this really be the case,
That a drop of Jesus' life-blood
Could all guilt and shame erase?
Could the sinner come confessing
Sins so evil one by one,
Be forgiven, cleansed and pardoned,
Find new life in Christ the Son?

If the blood be what atoneth
For the sins of those who come
To the throne of Mercy owning
They are lost and all undone;
Then what hinders them from coming,
What could make their hearts so cold?
To refuse so kind an offer
To deliver from sin's hold.

Oh, they're blinded by the devil,
That their eyes might never see
All the beauty in our Saviour,
Who's so real to you and me!
We must pray their eyes be opened,
Seek to warm their hearts to Him;
Tell of life and peace in Jesus,
God's blest answer for their sin.

Giving All to God

I oft have feared the cost involved
In giving all to God,
To live a life well-pleasing here,
Where once the Saviour trod;
Nought, nought I could in my strength tell,
Be gone, be gone, I bid farewell.
For were Thou not the strength to give
To loosen hold, let go to Thee,
I'd hold them close, would guard them dear,
And yet, more sad and empty be.

To say I am what I am not,
To say I'll do Thy bidding, Lord,
To say I'll go where none have gone,
To say I'll speak of Thy blest Word;
All, all are vain and empty talk,
If coming from unyielded will.
All, all would come to ruin, sure,
If Thou dost not this wish fulfill-

Of doing it Thyself in me
Creating what there ought to be
Giving sight that I might see,
And power to do what pleases Thee.

Let God take control!

Not Now

Not now, but soon, we'll see His face.
Not now, but soon be done this race.
The life of faith will soon be o'er:
We'll live with Him for ever more.

Today, not then, we learn His grace
Today, not then, His steps retrace.
We now appreciate His love
Who called our hearts to Him above.

Bless the Lord

Bless the Lord, who reigns on high.
He is worthy, this we cry.
Give Him glory, praise His name.
Tell His story, spread His fame.

Jesus lives, who once was dead;
Exalted high, the Church's Head;
For our sins was crucified:
See Him now the Glorified.

Soon He comes to take us home.
Jesus Lord, we beg Thee, come:
Long we've waited Thee to see.
Hearken now to this our plea.

Oh what joy will fill our heart,
Never more from Him to part!
When His welcome voice we hear,
Our loving Bridegroom will appear.

There's a Man in the Glory

There's a Man in the Glory,
Where none ever was,
And He lives interceding,
To plead for us;
Christ came down to earth as Man
To fulfill the Father's plan,
And to satisfy God's righteousness.

God so loved our sad world,
That He gave us His Son,
Born in Bethlehem-Judah
Of a virgin's womb;
And He lived a perfect life
In this world of sin and strife,
That God might be pleased with man again.

Man the Saviour rejected.
They cast that Man out;
Chose a thief who had murdered,
Away with Christ, they'd shout.
Then they nailed Him to a tree;
Jesus died for you and me,
And He shed His blood to purge our sins.

It is finished! He cried,
Then He bowed His blest head.
Christ, the Man of God's Counsel,
Now hung there dead;
Joseph placed Him in a tomb.
Soldiers sealed Him in that gloom:
God would have His dead put out of sight.

But He rose on the third day,
My Jesus arose!
Over sin now victorious,
He triumphed o'er His foes.
Now He lives the Church's Head.
To His saints, the living Bread,
Who sustains our souls until He comes.

There's a Man in the glory,
Where none ever was,
And He lives interceding,
To plead for us!

Could You Believe

Could you believe what God has done?
To save the world, He sent His Son.
Born of a virgin, came to earth;
The Father's heart He pleased from birth.

This Babe in favour daily grew,
And God His value fully knew.
The life He lived set Him apart,
And filled with joy the Father's heart;

Yet, God was pleased to make His Soul
A sacrifice to make us whole;
He bruised Him on the cross that day,
And as He bled, He turned away!

Our sins' full load was on Him laid:
The debt we owed, by Him was paid.
He cried in triumph, "All is done!"
The battle for my soul He won.

But, He was not left in the grave,
For there, my soul He could not save.
No! three days hence, my Lord arose,
To vanquish there my vilest foes!

We wait to see Him face to face,
The Lord who saved us by His grace;
He's coming soon, we have His word,
And we respond, "Come Jesus, Lord!!"

JOHN 3:16

For God so loved the world, that he gave his only begotten Son, that whosoever believeth in him should not perish, but have everlasting life.

The Lord is not ignorant of our suffering.

The Emptiness Inside is Real

The emptiness inside is real:
The Lord, Himself, knows how you feel.
Though others cannot enter in,
He fathoms all the pain within.

Alone He leads you through this trial,
With Satan's jeers, and mockings vile,
And well-meant words from those who care,
Who in a way your sorrows share.

In Christ we are united all,
And have a part in suffering's call.
So varied are the trials we face,
Yet, how sufficient is His grace.

To Him we cling, in this dark scene
Of heartaches oft, and foes so mean:
But soon we'll be in yon fair land,
As known, we'll know, and understand.

Love

With tongues of men and angels too,
And prophecy with knowledge fair;
Though faith were mine, and love were not,
E'en giving all, I'd be nowhere.

For love waits patiently in line
To see the Father's will revealed;
Is kind to all in all its ways,
And seeks not after greener fields.

Love puts itself not in the light,
And pride does not its ego fill;
Love never, ever misbehaves,
Nor seeks to satisfy its will.

A heart of love is not soon ired,
Though trials it may press so sore;
All thoughts of evil f leet away,
When Christ's love fills it more and more.

No joy is found at any sin,
But hearts rejoice at hearing truth.
Love bears all loads the Lord allows,
The yoke of Christ throughout its youth.

True love believes all that it's told,
Though some may seem as only tales;
It hopes in patience for all things,
For love endures and never fails.

Now faith abides, and hope, and love,
These three to which we have a call;
But of these is there one more dear?
'Tis love, the greatest of them all.

1 CORINTHIANS 13...

*...it takes a lifetime to learn,
And an eternity to fathom!!*

If I speak with the tongues of men and of angels, but do not have love, I have become a noisy gong or a clanging cymbal. If I have the gift of prophecy, and know all mysteries and all knowledge; and if I have all faith, so as to remove mountains, but do not have love, I am nothing. And if I give all my possessions to feed the poor, and if I surrender my body to be burned, but do not have love, it profits me nothing. Love is patient, love is kind and is not jealous; love does not brag and is not arrogant, does not act unbecomingly; it does not seek its own, is not provoked, does not take into account a wrong suffered, does not rejoice in unrighteousness, but rejoices with the truth; bears all things, believes all things, hopes all things, endures all things. Love never fails; but if there are gifts of prophecy, they will be done away; if there are tongues, they will cease; if there is knowledge, it will be done away. For we know in part and we prophesy in part; but when the perfect comes, the partial will be done away. When I was a child, I used to speak like a child, think like a child, reason like a child; when I became a man, I did away with childish things. For now we see in a mirror dimly, but then face to face; now I know in part, but then I will know fully just as I also have been fully known. But now faith, hope, love, abide these three; but the greatest of these is love.

In the Fullness of the Time

1

In the fullness of the time
God sent forth His Son,
That He might save sinners,
Lost and all undone;
Adam disobeyed God's voice,
Bringing sin and death;
Jesus Christ has paid the price
To save us every one.

CHORUS:

Come to Jesus Christ the Saviour,
God's own perfect Son;
See Him in the Glory,
Seated on His throne.

2

Could there be another
Like our blessed Lord?
Who could still the tempest
By His very word,
Who could touch a leper,
Cleanse and make him whole;
Heal the blind, the lame, the sick,
Be worshipped and adored.

(Chorus)

3
Are you heavy-laden,
Cumbered with much care?
Have you many burdens
You alone must bear?
Is there none to love you,
Comfort in distress?
Precious fact that you can take it
To the Lord in prayer!

(Chorus)

4
Has the blood of Jesus
Washed your sins away?
Has the Father's love
Taught your heart to say:
"I have peace and joy to know
Christ has saved my soul;
And He'll come to take me home
To live with Him alway"?

Come to Jesus Christ the Saviour
God's beloved Son;
See Him in the Glory,
Christ the living One!

JOHN 19: 30

When Jesus therefore had received the vinegar, he said, It is finished: and he bowed his head, and gave up the ghost.

It is Finished

It is finished. All is done.
Christ the victory hath won.
Ransomed now by God's blest Son,
Sing we praise to Him alone.

Not our labours could us save,
E'en we all our riches gave;
Nor the titles we may have
Follow us beyond the grave.

Flesh in any form is bad,
There's no good thence to be had.
Only One made God's heart glad-
Christ in human frailty clad.

Jesus Christ was born to die,
Ransomed such as you and I;
"It is finished", was His cry:
Sing we forth His victory.

"Loud Hosannas to the King!",
Freely may we ever sing.
Worship, praise and honour bring
Christ Who triumphed o'er death's sting.

Freed from all the curse of sin,
Life in Christ we now begin.
Spirit sealed, born from within –
Every battle His to win.

MARK 4:39

And he arose, and rebuked the wind, and said unto the sea, Peace, be still. And the wind ceased, and there was a great calm.

Jesus Will Not Fail Thee Ever

Jesus will not fail thee ever,
If thou dost His will desire.
Nought thee from His love can sever,
E'en when sinking in the mire.

Looking off to Him in glory,
In the deepest hour of need;
Be assured He will restore thee,
And thy cause in heaven He'll plead.

When the waves come crashing o'er thee,
And the load's too much to bear,
Give it to the Lord completely,
Casting on Him all thy care.

On thy knees is where to find Him,
Bringing all to Him in prayer;
In the closet thus reminded,
Death He suffered thee to spare.

Thus confiding in His Person,
Perfect, spotless, free from sin;
And His perfect work relied on
Frees thee from all doubt within.

In His love rejoicing ever,
Happy just to do His will,
Jesus from all fear will sever,
To thy storm say, "Peace, be still!"

MATTHEW 19: 4-6

And he answered and said unto them, Have ye not read, that he which made them at the beginning made them male and female, And said, For this cause shall a man leave father and mother, and shall cleave to his wife: and they twain shall be one flesh? Wherefore they are no more twain, but one flesh. What therefore God hath joined together, let not man put asunder.

Not Two, but One

Not two, but one;
Yet, still a pair:
A mystery, sure,
We'll fathom there.
Yet, while we're here,
Our lives are bound
With Christ, in love;
In Him we're found.

He gave us life
Through His shed blood,
Redeemed our souls
Back unto God;
He caused our lives
To touch one day,
Then worked it out
As we did pray.

Now here we are,
Both man and wife:
We're fellow heirs
Of the grace of life!

Oh Lord, Our Hearts Have Need of Peace

Oh Lord, our hearts have need of peace,
That we may walk in one accord.
Our wills, our ways, we now release,
And ask Thee to come in, O Lord.

Please help us to go on as one,
As in this scene we live for Thee:
Our hearts would cry "Thy will be done";
Oh help us now this will to see.

When with united hearts we walk,
The world would see Thy love displayed,
Be drawn as of Thy name we talk,
Convicted in their heart be made.

Then they, as well, would thus be led
To see their need of One so great;
Of Christ, the Lamb, whose blood was shed
Their sin and guilt, by death to take.

I Want to Go Home When It's Time

I want to go home with the rest of the crowd,
When it's time to go home to Thee;
And not because my heart never bowed
To Thy rightful authority.

My heart has resisted, and murmured and cried
'Gainst restraints You have placed in my life;
Forgetting, to save me from self-will, You died,
And release me from bondage and strife.

The days must be numbered, and closing up fast
Ere we hear Thy blest voice call us home:
So please grant me obedience and yielding, at last,
That I be not ashamed when You come.

If my self be not slain, nor my will lost in Thine,
Then in fear of Thy rod I shall live:
When instead I could walk in assurance divine;
Since my all in Thy care I did give,

I know not the way, nor the method, O Lord,
That will lead to this long-hoped-for end.
Please grant, through Thy Spirit, this grace to afford,
That Thy will I'd no longer contend.

PROVERBS 17: 3

The fining pot is for silver, and the furnace for gold: but the Lord trieth the hearts.

Oh to be Thankful

1
Oh to be thankful when all goeth ill,
To know that the Lord holds thy hand;
To know that He orders it after His will,
While leading thee into the land;
'Tis but for a moment, and soon will be o'er,
This time of great suffering and pain;
The weight of the glory is worth so much far more
Than all that this world could call gain.

CHORUS

Jesus knows best what's needed in each of our lives:
He sees what there lacks and out of His treasures He gives.
The joys and the sorrows both, they're all meant to bring us close;
He frees us from self, and closer to Himself He drives.

2
The fire it would separate silver from dross,
To prove it and make it reflect
The face of the finer, the Lord from the cross
Who thus would His own all perfect.
His love would permit neither wrinkle nor spot,
Nor blemish of sin or self-will;
All comes to the surface of His fining pot,
So be thankful when all goeth ill.

(Chorus)

1 THESSALONIANS 5: 16-18

Rejoice evermore.
Pray without ceasing.
In every thing give thanks: for this is the will of
God in Christ Jesus concerning you.

Give Thanks

Give thanks in the morning for mercies anew,
Give thanks for the Lord by thy side.
Give thanks that the Lord in His hands thee doth hide,
And leadeth thee all the day through.

Give thanks for the good and the evil as well,
Give thanks for the moments of peace;
Give thanks when the pressures and trials increase,
That thou hast a Saviour to tell.

Rejoice in the Lord now with all of your heart,
Give praise for the Father's blest Son;
Be thankful He saved you, and gave you a part
In the blessings, by dying, He won.

(Repeat vs 1)

It Couldn't be Long at All

No it couldn't be, wouldn't be, shouldn't be long,
It couldn't be long at all:
The Lord shall come and we shall rise
In answer to His call;

No it couldn't be, wouldn't be, shouldn't be long,
It couldn't be long at all:
The Lord shall come and we shall rise
In answer to His call;

The Lord shall come again,
Although we don't know when;
So let us read and pray,
That we'd be ready for that day;

For it couldn't be, wouldn't be, shouldn't be long,
It couldn't be long at all:
The Lord shall come and we shall rise
In answer to His call;

No, it couldn't be, wouldn't be, shouldn't be long,
It couldn't be long at all:
The Lord shall come and we shall rise
In answer to His call!

DO WE EAGERLY AWAIT CHRIST'S RETURN?

JOHN 10: 2-5

But he that entereth in by the door is the shepherd of the sheep. To him the porter openeth; and the sheep hear his voice: and he calleth his own sheep by name, and leadeth them out. And when he putteth forth his own sheep, he goeth before them, and the sheep follow him: for they know his voice. And a stranger will they not follow, but will flee from him: for they know not the voice of strangers.

Once I Was a Sinner

Once I was a sinner,
Lost in sin's control;
Then I met the Saviour,
Jesus made me whole.
Jesus died on Calv'ry,
All my sins forgave;
God raised Him to glory,
From the lowly grave.

Faith makes me a Christian,
Washed in Jesus' blood;
Heir of full salvation,
And a child of God;
Sinner won't you hearken,
To the Shepherd's voice?
Follow Him to heaven,
While you have the choice!

Forgetting That Which is Behind

Forgetting that which is behind,
I press toward the mark;
The prize of Christ my part to find,
When done this scene so dark;
The things that once were gain for me,
I now count loss for Christ;
That He might have supremacy,
Be won whate'er the price.

All that I lost I count but dung,
And more I would forego;
To gain the knowledge of my Lord,
His excellence to know;
My righteousness, when kept the law,
Could nought my soul avail:
'Twas filthy rags were all He saw,
When faith did not prevail.

My heart would long to know Him well,
His resurrection too;
The fellowship of sufferings tell,
Choice blessings ever new;
Conformed to His blessed death,
I wait to rise again;
That I may take that first sweet breath
In Heav'n, where Christ doth reign.

Not perfect, yet, I soon shall be,
And wait to lay firm hold
Of Him who apprehended me
For blessing yet untold;
Our calling is so very high,
Where Christ has gone before;
To bring us perfect by and by,
To peace for evermore!!!

PHILIPPIANS 3:7-16

*7 But what things were gain to me, those I counted loss for Christ.
8 Yea doubtless, and I count all things but loss for the excellency of the knowledge of Christ Jesus my Lord: for whom I have suffered the loss of all things, and do count them but dung, that I may win Christ,
9 And be found in him, not having mine own righteousness, which is of the law, but that which is through the faith of Christ, the righteousness which is of God by faith:
10 That I may know him, and the power of his resurrection, and the fellowship of his sufferings, being made conformable unto his death;
11 If by any means I might attain unto the resurrection of the dead.
12 Not as though I had already attained, either were already perfect: but I follow after, if that I may apprehend that for which also I am apprehended of Christ Jesus.
13 Brethren, I count not myself to have apprehended: but this one thing I do, forgetting those things which are behind, and reaching forth unto those things which are before,
14 I press toward the mark for the prize of the high calling of God in Christ Jesus.
15 Let us therefore, as many as be perfect, be thus minded: and if in any thing ye be otherwise minded, God shall reveal even this unto you.
16 Nevertheless, whereto we have already attained, let us walk by the same rule, let us mind the same thing.*

Round the Lord

Let's come together round the Lord,
And praise His holy Name,
Praise His holy Name,
Just praise His holy Name!
Let's come together round the Lord,
And praise His holy Name;
He is worthy of honour and of praise!

Jesus blesses His people,
Daily He loads us,
Richly He gives His children
More than they have room to take in:
Come together round the Lord
And praise His holy Name,
He is worthy of honour and of praise.

He is the Saviour,
Lord of creation,
King over all the earth,
He's coming soon to take us home!
Let's come together round the Lord,
And praise His holy Name,
He is worthy of honour and of PRAISE!!!

How I'm Doing

You ask me how I'm doing;
Do you really want to know?
Yes, the Lord is doing wonders,
But I've still so far to go.

It's not easy, but I'm trusting,
And the Lord is faithful, true:
He has promised grace abundant
For the trials He sees me through.

I've still a lot more lessons
To be learned along the way,
And He's promised more to teach me,
If I'll only trust and pray.

So, be sure to keep on asking;
There's so much that's going on:
If you want, I'll give you details
Of the battles we have won.

Soon the Lord will call us upwards
To our home in Heaven above;
But, till then, we learn His mercies
Through the leadings of His love!

Restored

She wandered away from the fold,
From the safety and warmth of the f lock,
Encountered a world dark and cold
Filled with those who the precious life stalk.

The wolf and the bear caught her scent,
Desiring a soul to consume;
On destruction and death they were bent,
For one more their desire had yet room.

The Shepherd on counting His sheep
Discovered He lacked now one lamb.
Not wanting to lose but to keep,
Went into the night with a lamp.

He sought and He sought for that one,
Whatever the cost it must be
Restored to the ninety and nine
Who prayed for its life on their knees.

Encountering the wolf and the bear
He found this poor lamb in their grasp;
Now downcast, and in great despair,
So repentant for all that had passed.

With a swing and a thud of His rod
He delivered that soul from their power;
Oh! the love of that blest Son of God
For His own was displayed in that hour.

The wounds she received went so deep,
But the Lord poured His oil and His wine;
And the love of her Lord for His sheep
Worked a healing more deep and divine.

The journey, as homeward they came
Was filled with rejoicing and praise;
No more would this lamb be the same,
Nor forget what He did all her days!

LUKE 15:4-7

4 What man of you, having an hundred sheep, if he lose one of them, doth not leave the ninety and nine in the wilderness, and go after that which is lost, until he find it? 5 And when he hath found it, he layeth it on his shoulders, rejoicing. 6 And when he cometh home, he calleth together his friends and neighbours, saying unto them, Rejoice with me; for I have found my sheep which was lost. 7 I say unto you, that likewise joy shall be in heaven over one sinner that repenteth, more than over ninety and nine just persons, which need no repentance.

Jesus Reigns

Jesus reigns supreme in glory,
Though unseen by man at large.
He the object is of myriads,
Who by faith their hearts engage;
'Tis a matter all transcending,
Ransomed souls their knees are bending.

See Him there our blessed Saviour!
God's beloved Man displayed.
He is worthy, and we worship:
Thus by God the Spirit led.
Soon He comes, His Church receiving,
Glad we wait, this word believing.

Take It to Him

Now I have to take it to the Lord,
I'll have to take Him at His word;
Believing that He's really heard
　　The pleadings of my heart;
　　To leave it at His feet,
　　That wondrous mercy seat,
　　Where God can with us meet,
　　And set apart.

There's a quiet place of rest and peace
Where burdened souls find sweet release
And wind and waves their raging cease,
　　When Jesus speaks the word;
　　The tempter flees away
　　When saints believing pray
　　And on His promise stay,
　　By faith assured.

Soon our faith will be turned into sight,
Our rags changed into robes of white,
God's cloudless day break through our night,
　　When Jesus calls us home:
　　We'll see Him face to face,
　　Who saved us by His grace,
　　And give to Him the praise;
　　LORD JESUS COME!!

Too Much

I could never understand it,
Just could never take it in,
Why the blessed King of glory
Took on Him my guilt and sin.

How could God, so just and holy,
Not condemn me where I stood,
Let me walk away a just man?
When He found in me no good.

'Tis a mystery I can't fathom,
But I praise Him that it's true;
Yes, He saved my soul completely,
He can do the same for you!

God looked down on fallen creatures,
Saw them lost and bound for hell,
Having turned from truth and justice,
Paths of life they'd known so well.

God said, I'll send my Son down,
He will bring them back to Me;
Jesus came a little baby,
Holy, blest nativity!

Mary's Son was very special:
Virgin-born by Spirit's power;
Son of God by declaration,
Destined for that very hour.

Jesus lived a perfect childhood,
As a man was perfect too;
God could call Him, My Beloved,
I have found delight in You!

Not a man before this Jesus
Gave such pleasure to God's heart,
Yet his life condemned the people,
So they forced Him to depart.

Man despised God's precious Love-gift,
Nailed Him to a shameful cross:
After scourgings, beatings, mockings
Man the fateful line did cross.

God was filled with indignation;
He must let His anger vent:
Yet instead of judging creatures,
All His wrath on Jesus went!

Yes! that sin demanded judgment,
As all others had before;
Yet, the sinless One did suffer
For that one and many more.

Only He who e'er was perfect
Could atone for sinners lost,
Being made what God detested:
Love would spare no pain or cost!

In those three long hours of darkness,
Left forsaken of His God,
Jesus bore eternal judgment,
While the world in darkness stood.

Then He breathed His last, and died there,
He who life eternal gives;
Buried, sealed, and watched for three days:
Yet, praise God, my Saviour Lives!

Yes! He rose to life a Victor
Over death and Satan too;
Now He lives in Heaven the Author
Of new life for me and you.

Yes, you too can know this Jesus
As your Saviour, Friend and Lord!
He is waiting now to save you,
Oh! please take Him at His word!

*Written in the mid 1980's
as a song of thanksgiving for God's redeeming grace.*

See Him There

See Him there in all His glory;
God's blest Son, oh what a story!
Never was a love like this.
Never was a life like His.

Came from heaven to earth to save us;
Oh! to think that God would have us,
In His presence, as His own,
And to know Him, as we're known.

Lived a life that pleased the Father,
Yet to die was willing rather,
That He might save us from sin,
Make us pure and clean within!

*What a Saviour we have there,
In the Glory!*

The Lord Doth Try the Hearts

The Lord doth try the hearts,
Their emptiness to prove:
He takes away the selfish pride,
Fills with His love;
He would not take away,
And leave us empty still;
With thoughts of Christ, and not of self
Our hearts would fill.

The Lord doth try the hearts,
As silver through the fire;
He looks to see Himself therein,
His heart's desire;
As gold the furnace proves,
And brings its brightness forth,
The trials and afflictions are
To prove new birth.

The Lord doth try the hearts
Of all His precious saints,
To drive us closer to His side
From all that taints;
He'd show the devil, too,
The power of His hand,
To keep from falling those He loves,
In this dark land.

The Lord doth try the hearts,
That we may know our frame,
And not rely on self for strength,
But on His Name;
He'd have us all to learn
To look to Him in all,
That we might stand in His great might,
And never fall.

JEREMIAH 17:9, 10

9 The heart is deceitful above all things, and desperately wicked: who can know it?
10 I the Lord search the heart, I try the reins, even to give every man according to his ways, and according to the fruit of his doings.

Peter's Words

O Lord, we fished all night,
And nothing could we catch;
But at Thy Word I'll drop the net,
I'm sure Thou knowest best.

O Lord, depart from me,
For I'm a sinful man:
But, at Thy Word, I'll follow Thee,
And fish for souls on land.

O Lord, if it be Thou,
Command to walk to Thee
Upon the water, where Thou art,
Though rough may be the sea.

O Lord, please save Thou me:
I'm sinking down through doubt.
The wind, the waves, the tempest, Lord,
Have moved my gaze from Thee.

O Lord, the strangers pay
The tribute to the King;
Thou said'st, "The children thus go free."
Our blessed lot with Thee.

O Lord, where can we go?
Thou hast the words of life.
Hence, we believe and are assured –
Thou art the Christ of God.

O Lord, thou are the Christ,
Son of the Living God.
Come down to build upon this rock
A church hell's gates won't move.

O Lord, Thou saidst to whom
This parable of Thine,
To us or all Thy servants now,
"Wait for your Lord and watch"?

O Lord, may God forbid
Thy suffering, shame and death;
It could not happen so to thee,
Such words I must rebuke.

O Lord, it's good for us
To be here in this place;
Let's make three dwellings here for Thee,
And both the prophets, too.

O Lord, the crowd doth throng
Thyself, and press Thee sore;
And sayest Thou," who touched Me now?"
'Twas not just one but more.

O see the fig tree, Lord,
Thou cursedst is dried up:
And saidst thou," Have the faith of God —
Nor doubt within your heart."

O Lord, declare to us
The meaning of this word;
"Not that which enters in defiles,
But what comes from the heart."

O Lord, we have left all
Behind and followed Thee.
What is the portion we shall have?
With Thee our greatest gain.

Lord, dost Thou wash my feet?
Oh, never let it be...
Not just my feet, but hands and head;
I'd have my part with Thee.

O Lord, where goest Thou —
Can I not follow now?
I'd lay my life down for Thy sake.
Thou knowest that I would.

O Lord, I'm set to go
With Thee to bonds and death;
Fret not Thyself o'er me at all;
My faith will never fail.

O Lord, I call to mind
Thy words so truly said:
"Before the cock crow twice Thou shalt
Me knowing thrice deny."

O Lord, Thou knowest all,
Thou knowest I love Thee.
Why hast Thou asked me these three times?
As though Thou doubtedst me.

O Lord, what of this man,
The one upon Thy breast;
I see him following after Thee —
What wilt Thou have him do?

The Perfect Life of Jesus Christ

The perfect life of Jesus Christ
Was such as all could see:
Yet, only to the eye of faith,
His Godhead Majesty;
'Twas only to a blessed few
He could reveal Himself —
The God of all eternity,
As Man, with men He dwelt.

The world could not His words receive:
Their ears were stopped by doubt.
Blind eyes His person ne'er perceived,
Whom prophets spoke about;
'Twas not the intellect could find
By wisdom of this world;
Nor could the disbelievers see,
Through miracles unfurled.

It took a simple childlike faith
To enter in at all
To things concerning life above,
The purpose of His call;
None else could ever do the work
That pleased the Father so.
All faith He gives this grace to see,
To them who Christ would know.

Christ Jesus came fresh life to give
To men by sin undone.
By dying on th'accursed cross
He all the victory won.
The perfect life of Jesus Christ
Was such as all could see:
Yet, only to the eye of faith,
His Godhead majesty.

1 CORINTHIANS 11:23-26

For I have received of the Lord that which also I delivered unto you, that the Lord Jesus the same night in which he was betrayed took bread: And when he had given thanks, he brake it, and said, Take, eat: this is my body, which is broken for you: this do in remembrance of me. After the same manner also he took the cup, when he had supped, saying, this cup is the new testament in my blood: this do ye, as oft as ye drink it, in remembrance of me. For as often as ye eat this bread, and drink this cup, ye do shew the Lord's death till he come.

These Emblems

We pass to one another
These emblems of Thy death,
In holy sweet communion:
Wish of Thy dying breath.
Our hearts are hushed in worship,
Rejoicing in Thy love,
And wait the day once promised-
To live with Thee above.

Stand Still

Stand still, be still, sit still:
These are the words of God.
Thus we see His great salvation,
Resting on His Word.

Stand still, be still, sit still:
Such wondrous words from Him;
Thus we can know that He is God,
Giving us peace within.

Stand still, be still, sit still:
His blessed voice we hear.
Thus we can see His great redemption.
There is no need to fear.

Stand still, be still, sit still:
Exalt Him in the earth.
Knowing for sure that He is God,
Spreading abroad His worth.

Stand still, be still, sit still:
In this we find our power.
No other name can bring deliverance,
In temptation's dreaded hour.

Stand still, be still, sit still:
His blessed voice we hear.
Salvation comes from God's own hand,
There is no need to fear.

Stand still, be still, sit still:
And know that He is God.
Exalt Him here upon the earth,
Where once the Saviour trod.

Stand still, be still, sit still:
In this our strength is found.
No other name deliverance brings
To those now homeward bound.

EXODUS 14 : 13

And Moses said unto the people, Fear ye not, stand still, and see the salvation of the Lord...

PSALM 46 : 10

Be still, and know that I am God...

ISAIAH 30 : 7 KJV

Their strength is to sit still.

Today's the Day

Today's the day to live for God:
We've life and breath and health.
He'll give us what we need for that,
Through Jesus' boundless wealth.

Be it to speak or help or show
Some kindness to a friend,
Or perfect strangers we've just met;
He'll bless it in the end.

There is no greater life than this,
No blessing from above,
Than letting others know He lives,
By sharing His great love!

We Fall Before Him

We fall before Him at His feet,
And give to Him all worship, praise.
There's none with Him that can compete:
He's worthy now, and all our days!
Soon, soon we'll see Him face to face,
Today we sing His matchless grace.

JOHN 14: 1-6

Let not your heart be troubled: ye believe in God, believe also in me. In my Father's house are many mansions: if it were not so, I would have told you. I go to prepare a place for you. And if I go and prepare a place for you, I will come again, and receive you unto myself; that where I am, there ye may be also. And whither I go ye know, and the way ye know. Thomas saith unto him, Lord, we know not whither thou goest; and how can we know the way? Jesus saith unto him, I am the way, the truth, and the life: no man cometh unto the Father, but by me.

The Lord Will Come

The Lord will come to take us home:
For this we have His word.
He's gone away until that day,
So think it not absurd,
That He will have the souls He saved,
His bride in white arrayed,
With Him above, to taste the love,
That our sins' debt once paid.

Roses in December

I saw roses in December,
Which the frost had not yet killed;
And the sun gleamed on their petals:
How my heart was awed and thrilled!

There were flowers in December
All around me blooming bright;
They were spared, but for a moment,
And I reveled in the sight.

Soon the cold of winter vanquished
Every flower, every bloom;
Nought was left but fondest memories,
And they stirred me through the gloom.

Onward trudging through the snow drifts,
Bent against the numbing blast,
Thoughts of blossoms in the spring-time
Made the winter pass by fast.

Oh, the sound of melting eaves troughs,
And the warming of the sun,
Speak of life in resurrection
To this winter-weary one.

There's a lesson to be learned here,
If our hearts would soon be taught:
What we face in life's tough moments,
Can with blessedness be fraught.

As a Beacon of Light

As a beacon of light and of hope,
In this dark evil world, help us Lord,
That we'd shine so that those who now grope
For the right Way, may see by Thy Word.

There's a darkness today we can feel,
As we walk through this wilderness here.
O please hearken, dear Lord, as we kneel,
For these lost souls to Thee are so dear.

Once in darkness we wandered as well,
Far from Thee in our blindness and sin:
But, Thy grace rescued our souls from hell,
And Thy Spirit shone Sonlight within.

Faith in Jesus has cleansed us from guilt!
God never a soul has denied,
Who their hope on His life-blood have built,
For, for their sakes on Calv'ry He died.

But He rose on the third day for us,
In triumph o'er sin and the grave;
Living now in such light glorious,
Waiting to receive those He has saved.

JAMES 5: 11

Behold, we count them happy which endure. Ye have heard of the patience of Job, and have seen the end of the Lord; that the Lord is very pitiful, and of tender mercy.

The Patience of Job

Remember the patience that Job had,
When suffering such things in his life:
Possessions and children were all lost,
His health, and the love of his wife.
Three friends tried to say he was sinning,
And that was the cause of his pain.
He cried to the Lord in his anguish,
And waited for His time for change.

As time passed he kept on defending
His self-righteous life in God's sight;
But there was no way He would have it:
Job just could not make himself right.
Elihu then spoke in their presence,
As one who knew God's perfect way;
Defending His wisdom in all things:
He left them with nothing to say.

The Lord spoke from Heaven in Job's ear:
He asked him to bring his defense.
But there were no words found to answer
God's wisdom and omnipotence;
The end of the Lord is so gracious:
Job did for his friends intercede.
And he was restored in his fortunes;
So blessed in the end, yes indeed!

You Know He's Jesus Christ

You know He's Jesus Christ
The Saviour of the world;
He lived a life well-pleasing here
To God the Father's heart;
He gave His life on Calvary
To save our souls from sin;
I love, I love, I love, I love Him so!

We love the Lord Jesus, don't we?

Some Handfuls of Purpose

Some handfuls of purpose the Lord ever leaves,
His choicest of blessings from out of the sheaves;
That that which we glean from the fields of His Word
May be a full measure, the faithful's reward.

Some handfuls of purpose, to lighten the task,
He ever would give us much more than we ask;
Though long may the day of our labours drag on,
No effort is fruitless when done for that One!

Some handfuls of purpose the Lord has in store,
To give to the needy, the hungry, the poor;
When seen that we're willing to leave all behind,
To trust and obey with a faith that is blind.

Some handfuls of purpose supplied for the way,
To give us our portion, our strength for the day;
The fruit of our labours, the choicest to have,
Remains when we beat out the grain from the chaff.

Some handfuls of purpose the Lord lets them fall,
Though we could not possibly gather them all;
There's plenty for us, and for others as well,
A bountiful harvest our hearts love to tell.

Some handfuls of purpose, the labour goes on,
The Lord of the harvest desires each one
To stay in the fields till the reaping is o'er,
And keep with His own, that the blessings be more.

Some handfuls of purpose, we all can rejoice:
Our hearts put to rest at our sweet Master's voice;
The Lord ever with you, while in this dark scene,
With handfuls of purpose, for those that would glean.

RUTH 2:13-18

13 Then she said, Let me find favour in thy sight, my lord; for that thou hast comforted me, and for that thou hast spoken friendly unto thine handmaid, though I be not like unto one of thine handmaidens.

14 And Boaz said unto her, At mealtime come thou hither, and eat of the bread, and dip thy morsel in the vinegar. And she sat beside the reapers: and he reached her parched corn, and she did eat, and was sufficed, and left.

15 And when she was risen up to glean, Boaz commanded his young men, saying, Let her glean even among the sheaves, and reproach her not:

16 And let fall also some of the handfuls of purpose for her, and leave them, that she may glean them, and rebuke her not.

17 So she gleaned in the field until even, and beat out that she had gleaned: and it was about an ephah of barley.

18 And she took it up, and went into the city: and her mother in law saw what she had gleaned: and she brought forth, and gave to her that she had reserved after she was sufficed.

Each Day in this Wilderness

Each day in this wilderness
Is one day closer home,
Where the Father will us bless
With riches yet unknown,
In a place prepared for us
By Christ Who went before,
That with Him we should be thus
As rich as He was poor.

For Christ walked this desert scene,
Was tempted of the foe,
Sorely suffered by man's hand,
His humanness to show;
But, through all remained the love
For sinners still undone,
Whom He'd bring to heaven above,
Co-heirs with Christ the Son.

Perfect He, and sin apart,
  He trod this dreary scene,
And revealed the Father's heart,
  Where He had ever been;
They who Him by faith believe
  Become the sons of God.
Life eternal they receive,
  Forgiveness in His blood.

Sinners once, now saints in Christ,
  The old is made full new.
By His beauty now enticed,
  What's past is dimmed from view.
Thus their journey has its course
  As heavenly people bound.
Each new day's a rich resource
  The depths of Christ to sound.

Each day we live brings us that much closer home!

We Walk by Faith

We walk by faith, and not by sight,
While in this scene so dark;
The Word of God our only light,
To guide us to the mark.
Where Christ has gone before us all,
To ready us a place;
The Father's house, our heav'nly call,
We who are saved by grace.

The journey is a per'lous one,
With many snares about;
The devil would us have undone,
And fill our hearts with doubt.
But, Christ our Lord is there to lead,
To glory up above;
Our souls would fully, richly feed,
With messages of love.

Though hard may be our pathway here,
All filled with grief and strife;
Our comfort is our Lord so dear,
Who gave His very life,
That we may by His Spirit led,
Find strength along the way;
And feed upon that living Bread,
Our Compass and our Stay.

We seek not rest nor peace below,
　　Our comfort is from Heav'n;
Thus ever would to Jesus go,
　　When by the tempest driv'n;
Our refuge when the foes attack,
　　A fortress in retreat;
He ever would us keep on track,
　　And gently wash our feet.

Soon will this vale of tears be o'er,
　　And we shall be with Him;
Rejoice in peace for evermore,
　　Our restless mem'ries dim;
The Master's voice, 'twill lift the heart,
　　As we to Him then fly;
Forever from this world depart,
　　At the archangel's cry.

Thus shall we ever with Him live,
　　In heavenly homes above;
Our hearts then would we fully give,
　　To fathom His great love;
Wherewith He counsel'd long before,
　　All things were ever made;
That we should be for evermore,
　　His bride in white arrayed!

Jesus Himself Shall Descend

The Lord Jesus himself shall descend
From His glorious throne up on high,
To call up His saints from the ends
Of the earth to Himself in the sky;
What glorious promise this holds
To every believer who longs
To be free from the pain that enfolds
Every heart to whom sorrow belongs.

He called us to faith and to love
Ere He went to the cross and its shame,
To abide till He called us above
In His love, and to pray in His name;
He who lived for the pleasure of God
Died condemned by the hatred of man,
And He willingly poured out His blood
That the gulf between both He might span.

Yes, He hung in our place on the cross,
There our guilt and our judgment He bore,
Was rejected by God then for us,
That we might be free evermore!
Once bound to this world and its course
We've been brought into heavenly things;
This causes our hearts to rejoice
And daily His praises to sing!

1 THESSALONIANS 4:13-18

But I would not have you to be ignorant, brethren, concerning them which are asleep, that ye sorrow not, even as others which have no hope.

For if we believe that Jesus died and rose again, even so them also which sleep in Jesus will God bring with him.

For this we say unto you by the word of the Lord, that we which are alive and remain unto the coming of the Lord shall not prevent them which are asleep.

For the Lord himself shall descend from heaven with a shout, with the voice of the archangel, and with the trump of God: and the dead in Christ shall rise first:

Then we which are alive and remain shall be caught up together with them in the clouds, to meet the Lord in the air: and so shall we ever be with the Lord.

Wherefore comfort one another with these words.

United

With Jesus on high we're united:
It's from there that the victory's won;
No need to be sad or affrighted:
For we're children beloved as the Son!
With our eyes on Him there
In the glory so fair,
We're assured that the vict'ry is ours;
When we call on His name,
He who's always the same
Will rescue us from Satan's powers.

The battle's not ours, but the Saviour's,
For we never could fight on our own;
It's not by our feeble endeavours,
But by His mighty power alone!
He who gave us His life
Is aware of the strife
That is found upon entering the land;
Every step that we take
He has promised to make
A blessing received from His hand.

Let's fear not to take our possessions,
As we have them in Jesus our Head.
Though compassed by sore tribulations,
We're assured that through all we'll be led.
Soon the battles all done
We'll be brought to the Son
To be with Him always as His bride;
Oh what joy it will be
His glory to see,
And ever with Him to abide!

Let's keep looking to Jesus,
The Author and Finisher of our faith!

Victory

I cannot walk another step
Along this weary road,
Unless, by grace, I can accept
The sovereign ways of God.

I can't take one more step along
This pathway that I'm on,
If Christ be not my joy and song
Till pilgrim days be done.

Continue on I must, I must
Whatever be the cost;
God must be God, and very just,
Else heart and mind be lost.

The en'my wages war each day,
Satan, the flesh, the world;
I must let Christ have sovereign sway,
And wait His ways unfurled.

Oh, that the vict'ry might be had
By casting all on Him;
For if He rules, can I be sad,
E'en if the way grow dim?

For if the heart be firmly set
On Christ exalted high,
My faith can grow much stronger yet,
As on HIM I rely!

Faith

Faith then comes by hearing,
And hearing by the Word of God;
The gospel of God's mercy
Sealed in Jesus' blood;
But who will preach the message
Of a Saviour's love,
Who saw the world in danger
Of vengeance from above?

God sent His dear Son Jesus
Down to this world of woe,
Who veiled His Godhead glory,
And walked as Man below;
He preached the blessed gospel
Of God's redeeming grace
Of free and full salvation
For those who'd seek His face.

.Man heard, but spurned the message,
And turned a stiffened neck,
Refused their souls' salvation,
And chose their lives to wreck!
They called not for forgiveness,
They chose to crucify
The Christ their own Messiah,
Who willingly did die.

Oh Lord of the great harvest
Please send the lab'rers out,
That they may preach the Gospel
To those who live in doubt.
Do let their ears be opened,
Their hearts give to believe;
And hear them when they call Thee,
As Thy Word they receive!

ROMANS 10:9-17

ROMANS 10:9-17

That if thou shalt confess with thy mouth the Lord Jesus, and shalt believe in thine heart that God hath raised him from the dead, thou shalt be saved. For with the heart man believeth unto righteousness; and with the mouth confession is made unto salvation. For the scripture saith, Whosoever believeth on him shall not be ashamed. For there is no difference between the Jew and the Greek: for the same Lord over all is rich unto all that call upon him. For whosoever shall call upon the name of the Lord shall be saved. How then shall they call on him in whom they have not believed? and how shall they believe in him of whom they have not heard? and how shall they hear without a preacher? And how shall they preach, except they be sent? as it is written, How beautiful are the feet of them that preach the gospel of peace, and bring glad tidings of good things! But they have not all obeyed the gospel. For Esaias saith, Lord, who hath believed our report? So then faith cometh by hearing, and hearing by the word of God.

MATTHEW 7: 14

Because strait is the gate, and narrow is the way, which leadeth unto life, and few there be that find it.

Take Heart

It's such a narrow path we tread,
When we to self-will would be dead:
But Christ our blessed Lord has said,
    Take heart, you're not alone.

Sometimes we find ourselves alone;
The path had only room for one.
Though dark may be the road we've gone,
    Take heart, He leads the way.

We find it such a trying way
We walk along from day to day,
With Christ our only help and stay,
    Take heart, He gives a song.

He gives a song to help us through,
When we don't know just what to do:
And proves in us His word is true,
    Take heart, He's coming soon.

He's coming soon to take us home;
Then we this path no more shall roam.
The Spirit and the bride say, "Come!"
    Lord Jesus, tarry not.

1980's Plea

Make me to be
What You want me to be,
And help me to be in the good-
Of all that was done,
When You died all alone
On the cross
Where You poured out Your blood.

Quickly scribbled on a card as thoughts came, while working for Canada Post (as were many other poems)

2 CORINTHIANS 12: 9

And he said unto me, My grace is sufficient for thee: for my strength is made perfect in weakness. Most gladly therefore will I rather glory in my infirmities, that the power of Christ may rest upon me.

Thou art Enough

Thou art enough Lord Jesus Christ
For all our care or need;
Thy grace it always doth suffice.
Thy presence cheers indeed.

'Tis not just in the times of want
We sense Thy tender care;
No, e'en when psalms and hymns we chant,
Lord Jesus, Thou art there!

Such Thy Love to Me

Waters deeper than I've ever seen,
Fires hotter than they've ever been,
Such Thy love to me;
Foes more cruel than I've ever known,
Paths more rugged than I've ever gone,
Such Thy love to me;
Ever hast Thou been the same,
Depths of water, heat of flame,
Ever faithful to Thy name,
When cruelest foes across my pathway came.

Highest mountains looming in my way,
Darkest hours of my longest day,
Such Thy love to me;
Deepest valleys in my lowest hour,
Weakest moments facing Satan's power,
Such Thy love to me;
Ever hast Thou led the way,
Highest mountains, darkest day,
Ever Thou my help and stay,
When I'd to Thee in deepest weakness pray.

Richest blessings o'er my life have come,
Greatest promise of a heavenly home,
Such Thy love to me;
Peace much deeper than my heart takes in,
Grace much greater than my blackest sin,
Such Thy love to me;
Only Jesus Christ, God's Son
Has this all on Calv'ry won.
Only He the work has done.
He'll complete in us what He's begun!

ISAIAH 43: 2

When thou passest through the waters, I will be with thee; and through the rivers, they shall not overflow thee: when thou walkest through the fire, thou shalt not be burned; neither shall the flame kindle upon thee.

ACTS 11: 26

And when he had found him, he brought him unto Antioch. And it came to pass, that a whole year they assembled themselves with the church, and taught much people. And the disciples were called Christians first in Antioch.

Christians First

Christians first they called them there
In Antioch, I heard.
Their lives did such a witness bear
Of Christ and His blest Word.
A few believers bound in love
To one another's lives,
United to their Head above,
Through grace the Saviour gives.

1 TIMOTHY 1: 15

This is a faithful saying, and worthy of all acceptation, that Christ Jesus came into the world to save sinners; of whom I am chief.

Jesus Came

Jesus came to earth to die
For lost sinners;
Now He lives to intercede
For believers;
Soon He'll come to earth again;
Let's be watching, ready then,
That He find us true and faithful
At His coming.

He who came to earth before
Shall return once more!
Let's be faithful, watching, ready
At His coming;
He will call His bride away
To eternal Day!
Let's be faithful, watching, ready
At His coming.

Repeat verse one

To Those Who Wait on God

To those who wait on God
He always gives the best.
It isn't always easy, but
We know it's blest.
We leave the choice to Him,
Who doeth all things well.
In patience wait His will to know;
His time will tell.

When we make God's will our will,
-We're assured the Lord will bless the outcome,
In His time

Oh Lord, You Know I Need You

Oh Lord, You know I need you.
You know I really do.
And if I were without You,
Oh Lord what would I do?
My life and breath are in Your hand;
For by your grace alone I stand.
Please lead me through this barren land,
Until I'm home with You.

John MS Neufeld
1987

Faithful Warriors

They fought so valiantly together,
Side by side against the foe.
Men of valour in the battle;
Faithful to the death they go.

Leaving all to serve their country,
Knowing not if they'll return.
Family, friends, their loved ones waiting,
While sad eyes with watching burn.

Through the ages duty called them,
To defend their lands so fair.
Thanks to them for all their efforts,
All who arms in battle bear.

John MS Neufeld
24 May 2006

Oh Wretched Man that I Am

Oh wretched man that I am,
If left to my own device.
But I thank God through Christ Jesus,
The Lord who gives me peace.

Woe is me, I'm undone.
I have seen a thrice-holy God;
Yet out from the altar, O blessed news!
Thy sin has been purged by His blood.

I abhor myself, seeing Thee now,
And in dust and ashes I fall.
Yet, I hear from Thy lips a mystery sure:
I'll hear you, when on me you call.

"Tis not by my efforts or will,
Or a self-righteous view of myself;
But a looking to Jesus, the author of faith,
And the One who will finish, Himself!

John MS Neufeld
03 January 2000

Oh Lord, We Long to Follow Thee

Oh Lord, we long to follow Thee,
To bear Thy likeness more.
Be found before our journey ends;
Reflections of our Lord.

And yet, we know 'twill cost us dear
To have this brought about.
We're called to give our lives to Thee:
For us there's no way out.

So take us as we are, dear Lord,
Conform us to Thy will.
Create in us clean hearts prepared
Thy bidding to fulfill.

Remove the stumbling blocks, we pray,
The walls we've built, tear down.
Our secret sins expose, that they
No more obscure Thy throne.

That throne of mercy and of grace
To which we're called to come;
In perfect liberty to bring
All we find troublesome.

For if our hearts are burdened down,
And robbed of peace and joy,
'Tis hard to lift the feeblest prayer,
Or songs of praise employ.

Yet, once we yield it all to Thee,
And find Thy sweet release,
'Tis then our hearts are filled with praise
We wish would never cease.

So help us every day, we pray
To spend that time alone;
Shut up awhile in fellowship
With Thee upon the throne.

For only then could we expect
To face each coming day
With power and grace and confidence
From Thee, our Help and Stay.

We're needy people, Lord we are,
We own it in our hearts.
Dependent on Thee all the while,
For strength Thy grace imparts.

Oh let us short accounts maintain
With God and fellow men:
A conscience purged of guilt, for we
Confessed it there and then.

We bless Thee for Thy faithfulness,
The kindness to us shown;
Of peace with God enjoyed on earth,
Of full redemption known.

John MS Neufeld
29/30 December 1990

The Storm May Full be Raging

The storm may full be raging,
The tempest blast without:
I'll stay with Thee, my refuge,
And not be tossed about.
I know no safer covert,
There is no higher ground;
'Tis Thou my blessed Saviour
Who keeps me safe and sound.

The wintry chill of dying
May hold me in its power;
I've not to fret nor worry.
'Twill be my finest hour.
My Jesus is the victor
O'er death and Satan's sting.
He fills my heart with praises,
And sweetest peace doth bring.

Alone and in affliction,
He is my hiding place.
Whate'er without may threaten,
He keeps me by His grace.
Though oft the path be weary,
All rife with grief and pain,
I have no need for doubting
Nor cause yet to complain.

This wilderness is empty
Of aught which satisfies.
The gilt of all its treasures
Would from Christ draw my eyes.
I'll ask Him for my soul's needs,
Seek comfort from His Word;
Knock at His doors of promise,
Where all true treasure's stored!

John MS Neufeld

How He Leads Them On

He led them on by His skilful hands
Through mighty seas and sun-parched lands
Laid down for them His just commands.
Yes, how He led them on!

From Abel's time to the present day,
Living by faith has been the way.
Though the cost be all, e'en our life to pay;
Oh Lord, please lead us on!

Through the mighty swells of a fearful storm
Noah's household was kept safe and warm:
In the Ark of God he would fear no harm.
Oh still He led them on!

Abram left all he had for God.
As a pilgrim far from home he trod,
Felt the faithful Shepherd's staff and rod.
Still, while He led them on!

In the promised land he and his did roam,
With nary a place to call his home.
E'en Sarah conceived in her barren womb.
Oh, how He led them on!

His son he was asked to freely give;
That one through whom his name would live;
Yet, he this promise did receive:
Now will I lead thee on!

Some years had passed, and the nation grew
Mighty and great; they were not a few.
Yet in bondage to Egypt, just what could they do?
Surely He'd lead them on!

Moses would spend forty years in the courts
Of Egypt oft hearing his people's reports.
Then still forty more, Midian's shepherd of sorts.
There, where He led him on!

Now the people were ready to go on their way
From their bondage and service, they did not delay.
With their Passover finished, their hearts could now say,
See how He leads us on!

The journey was fraught with much danger, you see.
But by God's deliverance, His people were free
To serve Him, His own prized possession to be.
And faithfully still leads them on!

John MS Neufeld

What if the Lord Should Come Before?

What if the Lord should come before
I to my wedding go?
Our lives then never joined as one;
No future here below.
Should thoughts of this distress my mind,
I've purposed what to do:
To praise and glorify the Lord
For all He's brought us through.

The days are few and treacherous;
His coming near at hand
To call His bride away to Him
To that yon glorious Land.
Where we shall stand in robes of white,
Our Bridegroom at our side;
Be joined to Him with cords of love,
His heart then satisfied.

We'll spend eternity with Him,
Who died to save our souls,
And rose again; our sins atoned.
Whose love our heart controls.
Our lives then only just begun:
The sweetest time of all.
The Bridegroom and His Bride at last
In purest love enthralled!

John MS Neufeld
1991/1992

The Old Testament Books

In those five books of Moses,
God sets His standard high:
From first to last He shows to man
Their need, and His supply.
In Joshua and in Judges too
The stage is set for war
Against a host of enemies
Whose ways would try them sore.

Dear Ruth is such a simple book
Of God's great love and grace;
A castaway and widow, too,
In blessing finds her place.
First and Second Samuel,
Then Kings and Chronicles
Reveal the ways of God with those
Who'd slight His principles.

Ezra, Nehemiah, Esther
Recovery is their theme.
The Temple, walls and even life
Restored by power supreme.
Job would lose what he held dear;
Yes, e'en his wife's support.
Then by his friends be charged with sin;
For this by God abhorred.

There's poetry and prose divine
Beheld within the Psalms.
While Proverbs and the Preacher too,
Give wisdom from Heavenly realms.
Song of Solomon's about
The love of two so great;
That, though the urge of both was strong,
God's timing they would wait.

Isaiah speaks the mind of God;
Jeremiah tells the heart :
While in the book of Lamentations
There's a rending of that heart.
Ezekiel shows the glory
Of the Lord departing up
From the city, where dwells His Name
For His people were corrupt.

Daniel, though a captive
In a far off land,
With his friends oft proved the power
Of their great Saviour's hand.
Hosea shows a faithful heart
To one who's so untrue;
Like the way the Lord would labour
With such as me and you.

The prophets paint a picture
Of a people and their God:
They unfaithful, He so patient
Using staff and rod.
Our Old Testament is helpful
In learning God's blest ways.
Let's enjoy it, read it, trust it,
Our remaining days!

John MS Neufeld
26 September 1997

COVID's For Real. Eternity, Too!

We really have to wait this out,
Of that there truly is no doubt.
It took the world by storm, it did,
A germ of which we'd all be rid;
A cure for which the nations bid,
Which leaders fret about.

It came across the seas one day,
From Wuhan city far away.
It spread across the world so fast,
Some thought it just some days would last,
Now half a year or more has passed:
Most think it's here to stay.

So what to do while thousands die?
Should we stand simply idle by?
By no means, no! There's work to do.
A task for me, a job for you.
We'll not be done till this is through.
Be brave, I'll tell you why.

The first responders have their task.
We too can duly don a mask,
And all can keep six feet apart,
Though this may seem a feeble start.
Simple deeds done from the heart:
Enough? I hear you ask.

When called to work, or to stay home,
Asked not the streets en masse to roam:
We'll be responsible, you bet,
'Cause we don't want this bug to get.
It's not our friend, nor e'en a pet.
This pest we're keeping from.

Be ready now to meet your God,
Trust in the Saviour's precious blood.
None knows for sure how they'll respond,
If they'll get through it safe and sound,
Or if succumbing, on what ground
Their souls have ever stood.

There's rest and peace and joy and love,
In Jesus Christ in Heav'n above.
He came to set our souls at ease.
Yes He the Father's heart did please.
His blood avails for each of these,
Their sins' guilt to remove.

So come today, why linger now?
Lis-ten to me, I'll tell you how:
If you would live with confidence,
Know your eternal residence,
It's Jesus makes the differ-ence.
To Him in peace you'll go!

John MS Neufeld
14 May 2020

www.ingramcontent.com/pod-product-compliance
Lightning Source LLC
LaVergne TN
LVHW021717060526
838200LV00050B/2708